Careers in Wearable Electronics

Martin Gitlin

Published in the United States of America by
Cherry Lake Publishing, Ann Arbor, Michigan
www.cherrylakepublishing.com

Reading Adviser: Marla Conn, MS, Ed., Literacy specialist, Read-Ability, Inc.

Photo Credits: Cover, BsWei; page 4 (left), eHrach; Page 4 (right), Riksa Prayogi; page 6, Africa Images; page 8, Willyam Bradberry; page 10, Andrey Popov; page 12, Anna Ieni; page 14, Gorodenkoff; page 16, aurielaki; page 18. Alexey Boldin; page 20, Macrovector; page 22, Beros919; page 24, Dima Sidelnikov; page 26, Rawpixel.com; page 28, Andrey_Popov. Source: Shutterstock.

Library of Congress Cataloging-in-Publication Data

CIP data has been filed and is available at catalog.loc.gov.

Printed in the United States of America.

Table of Contents

Hello, Emerging Tech Careers!

In the past ...

Groundbreaking inventions made life easier in many ways.

In the present ...

New technologies are changing the world in mind-boggling ways.

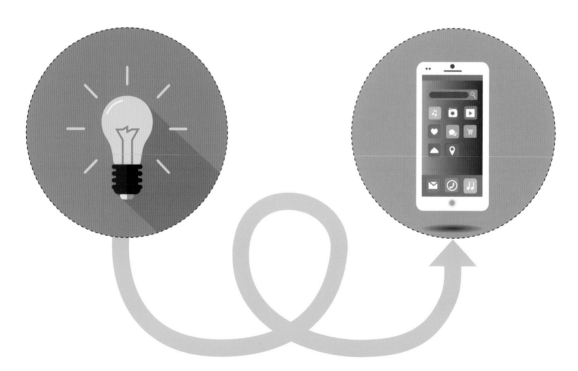

The future is yours to imagine!

WHAT COMES NEXT?

Who would have thought?

Alexander Graham Bell invented the first telephone in 1876. In 1879, Thomas Edison invented the first electric lightbulb. The Wright brothers successfully flew the first airplane in 1903. And don't forget Henry Ford! He invented a way to make cars quicker and cheaper.

These brilliant inventors did things that people once thought were impossible. To go from candles to electricity? From horse-drawn carriages to automobiles and airplanes? Wow!

The sky's the limit!

Now technology is being used to do even more amazing things! Take **wearable electronics**. These smart electronic devices can be worn on the body as an implant or accessory. FitBits are a popular example of this type of technology. These devices monitor a wearer's activity, exercise, food, weight, and sleep for health purposes.

This book explores the people and professions behind wearable technology. Some of these careers, like AI programmer, are so cutting-edge that they didn't exist just a decade or so ago. Others, like data analyst, offer exciting new twists using wearable technology.

Read on to explore exciting possibilities for your future!

Artificial Intelligence Programmer

They take a collection of parts and codes and bring them to life. **Robots**? Video games? **Wearable technology**? These tools are dead without the work of artificial intelligence (AI) programmers. They program technology to think and communicate in human-like ways. This career is the wave of the future.

Their work is critical to robotics and wearable technology. Their career title fits perfectly. They indeed bring intelligence to programs and equipment. And they now create what was science fiction a short time ago.

Systems they develop perform tasks that normally require human intelligence. Among them are **visual perception**, speech recognition, and decision-making.

AI programmers contribute greatly to modern technology. They have changed everything from transportation to social media to online shopping to gaming. And their effect on wearable technology has been huge.

It has greatly impacted wearables related to health and sports. One example is a headgear for swimmers that count their strokes. It measures efficiency in body movement. Another is a wristband that judges a boxer's technique.

AI programmers have done amazing things with smart watches. Included are devices that read health levels during

Imagine It!

➡ Imagine in your mind what a robot you created would look like.

➡ Think about your least favorite chore at home.

➡ Now draw a picture of your robot doing that chore for you.

Dig Deeper!

✔ Use your favorite web browser (like Google) to search online for "the best wearable tech games and toys for kids".

✔ Make a list of what cool features each of those futuristic games and toys can do.

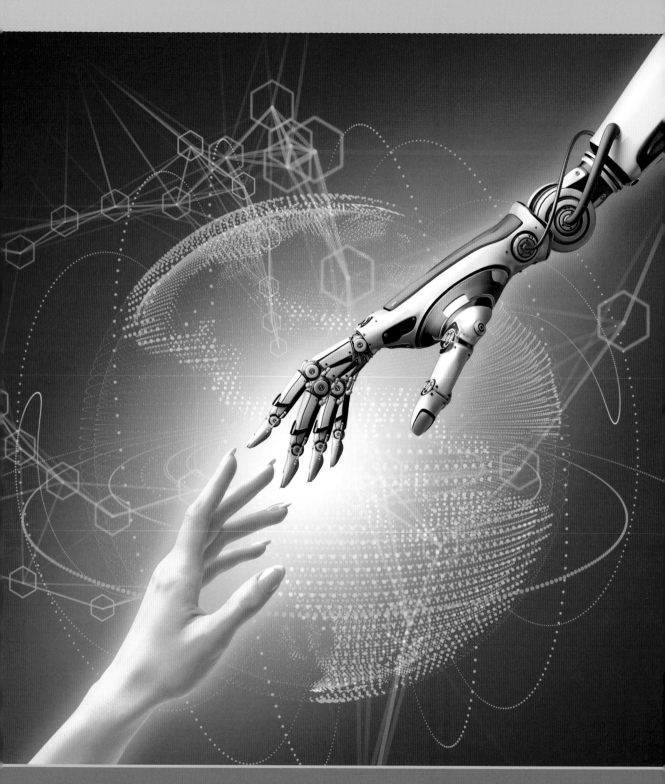

Human intelligence is needed to make smart computers and machines.

arguments! They read skin temperature and blood pressure. They combine this data with audio of the verbal battle to determine how arguments affect health.

Wearable games depend on experts in this field. They program game bands, headsets, watches, and even shoes that communicate with each other. They can also program wearables that connect with computers and tablets. The result is fun and futuristic games played inside or outside.

AI programmers have already influenced society. They have programmed smartphones to give verbal directions to drivers. They have created filters that kill off spam emails. They have developed ways to deposit checks through smartphones. This makes banking much easier for families like yours.

Artificial intelligence programmers are super smart technology professionals. It takes strong math and computer skills to design and develop the really cool AI software that they work on.

Future AI Programmer

Those who wish to pursue even beginning AI programming work must earn a college degree. Common fields of study include computer science, robotics, and engineering. They should also gain training and experience in programming languages. Among them is Java.

Data Analyst

In all businesses, someone has to crunch the numbers. This person has to understand the industry and make predictions. Will his or her company succeed or fail? This is the job of data analysts. The discoveries they make play a big role in determining the future of companies that make wearable electronics.

Data are facts and information used to calculate and analyze. Analysts find and gather data. They organize it and use it to reach conclusions. Companies in nearly every industry hire data analysts.

Data analysts help businesses make critical decisions. They answer many questions. What should they sell? How much of a product should they produce? What should they charge for that product? What group of people are most and least likely to buy it? How much profit should they expect to earn?

The work of data analysts centers on **consumer** habits. They answer questions like: What types of wearable products do consumers want and need? How can this technology be used to solve a problem or create some fun? What is the most comfortable way to wear technology?

Data analysts also use information to predict what consumers will buy. They look at disposable income – the amount of money people have for things they want but don't necessarily need.

Imagine It!

→ Pretend you are a data analyst researching a game you enjoy.

→ Consider what you like about the game. But also think about how it can be improved.

→ Create a two-sided chart that lists its positives and negatives.

Dig Deeper!

✔ Check out the following website: http://www.softschools.com/math/data_analysis.

✔ Pretend you are a data analyst as you work through the different activities.

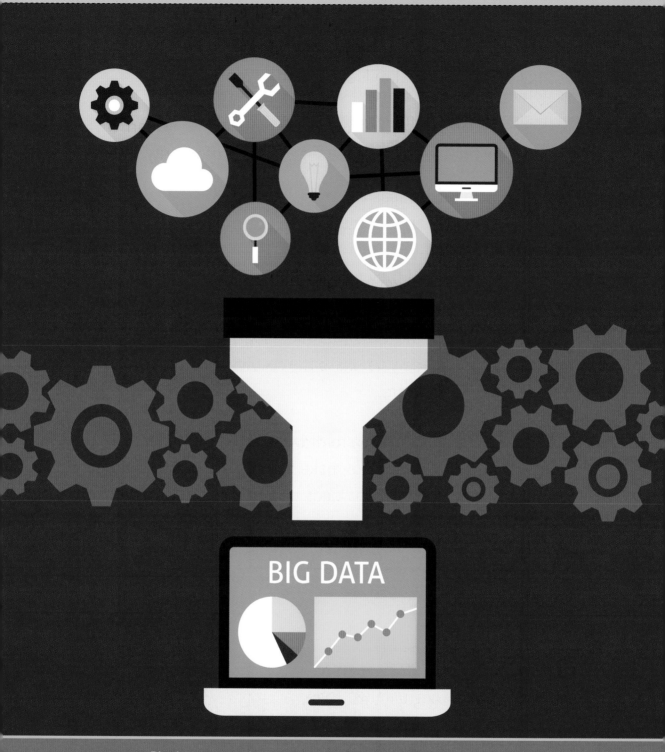

Big data means that data analysts gather lots of information from lots of different sources.

Wearables are often bought for fun or to improve quality of life. But they aren't essential to life like food or rent.

Those that analyze data look for buying patterns. They learn if certain kinds of products are gaining or losing popularity. Then they use data to figure out why.

Data analysts do not work alone. They are part of team that includes the people responsible for creating new products and selling them. The team works together to decide what kinds of information they need to create or improve a product. They figure out what they need to know about the people most likely to buy their product. Data analysts share the results of their research with other team members.

Data analysts use information to draw conclusions and make recommendations. They do not make the final decisions. But their work helps others decide what kinds of wearable technology to create next.

Future Data Analyst

Data analysts take courses in information technology and **statistics**. They generally must earn a bachelor's degree to enter the field. But some companies require even more college training called master's degrees. Data analysts need skills in math and analytics. They should also become familiar with computer programming.

Game Developer

They can be worn on the wrist or head or feet. They can be created for children, teens, or adults. They can have you sitting down or running around. They can be enjoyed inside or outside.

They are toys and games of the present and future. And *they* are the creations of wearable game developers.

The basic idea behind playing games has not changed for centuries. Game developers still ask the same question. What would people like to play?

Thanks to technology, the way people play games has changed a lot. Games started getting more complex decades ago. First there were simple board games like Monopoly and Scrabble. Then there were video games such as Pac-Man and Space Invaders. Computer games later gained popularity.

But time and technology march on. And game developers are creating a new wave of fun. They are producing wearables that promise to flourish in the future. They use their imaginations to invent creative games. They figure out what consumers crave. And they are tech savvy enough to develop games that will sell.

Developers create toys that expand the mind. One popular example is the **virtual reality** headset. Those that wear them can do everything from deliver a baby elephant to walk in space.

Imagine It!

→ Think about any outdoor game or sport you enjoy playing.

→ Now imagine how you could add a wearable that would make it more fun or challenging.

→ Play the game as if you had strapped on the wearable and it could do whatever you wanted.

Dig Deeper!

✓ Go online to https://scratch.mit.edu.

✓ Click on the "create" button to create your own game.

✓ Click on the "explore" button to explore games created by kids from all over the world.

Teams of talented professionals develop fun games.

One takes users to the planet Jupiter. Another places them into the role of detective in a murder mystery.

Other devices developers dreamed up require only a wrist and smartphone or tablet. For instance, one type of slap-on bracelet encourages kids to move around and be active. It creates realistic sounds based on the movements. It makes waving a stick sound like brandishing a sword or tapping a pencil sound like playing drums.

Developers have invented watches with still and video cameras. They feature a recorder, voice changer, alarm, timer, stopwatch, calendar, and calculator! Another allows young children to take care of a virtual pet while getting exercise.

Even shoes have been transformed into games. They come with a remote control and feature lights and sounds that keep kids active.

Future Game Developer

Some game developers need only a high school diploma and lots of computer know-how. But many game studios require a college degree. One must also gain experience working in computer science, programming, or art. Creativity and the willingness to work with others are a must. So is understanding programming languages and software programs.

Hardware Engineer

Inside all computers—and wearable technologies—are things like processors, circuit boards, memory devices, networks, and routers. These are called **components**. They are the parts that make technology work. The components inside wearable technologies might be very small but they are very powerful.

Nobody can perfectly predict the future of wearable technology. It is even hard to forecast what will be created next. But one thing is certain. Whatever it is, a hardware engineer will be called upon to turn that idea into reality.

It takes two kinds of engineers to create wearable technology. Hardware engineers are responsible for anything you can touch. That means the watch or device itself. Software engineers are responsible for programming the systems that make the technology work.

Hardware engineers have designed devices that can improve or even save lives. Among them is a device that sends energy waves into the wrist to destroy cancer cells. The patient takes a pill that marks the diseased cells before the device goes to work.

Smart watches and fitness trackers gained the greatest success. Smart watches do far more than tell time. They run apps and allow users to play music or radio on headphones. Some also have

Imagine It!

➡ Imagine you are a hardware engineer.

➡ You are given the choice of designing a new smart watch or a product that could help medical patients.

➡ Write down what you would like and dislike about both options.

Dig Deeper!

✔ Read all about the FitBit here: https://electronics.howstuffworks.com/gadgets/fitness/fitbit.htm.

✔ List all the ways people can use FitBit.

Smart Accessory
Security

RunningWatch

Smart Glass

Activity Trackers

Tablet Computer

Smart Sneakers

MP3 Player

Digital Book

Healthcare Devices

Portable Games

Smartphone

SmartWatch

MP3 Player

Digital Camera

SmartWatch

Smart Camera

Hardware engineers create many different types of wearable technologies.

touch screens. That results in functions such as calculators and compasses. They can also bring up the Internet. That means users can receive emails and text messages through their smart phones.

Products such as the FitBit have allowed users to become more active, eat and sleep better, and improve their health. The FitBit is just two inches long. It can be attached to the body or placed in a pocket. It logs a range of data about daily activities. Included are steps taken, distance traveled, and calories burned. The FitBit also monitors how well one sleeps. It knows when users go to bed and how often they wake up during the night.

Hardware engineers are just scratching the surface of their potential. Their usefulness to the future of wearable technology cannot be understated.

Future Hardware Engineer

Most entry-level hardware engineers gain a college degree in computer engineering. But one in electrical engineering is often fine as well. Students must be strong in math and science to succeed in this field. A background in computer programming is also generally required. Schools sometimes offer internships that provide job experience. Some companies require hardware engineers to earn a master's degree in computer engineering.

Marketing Director

What *is* this wearable technology all about? What does it do? How does it work? Why would it be fun and helpful to users? What is the best way to explain all that to people? These are the types of questions marketing directors ask themselves everyday. The answers they find help them sell wearable technology products to the people who want and need them.

Wearables can be tough for people to understand. The technology is advanced. Their uses are difficult to grasp. They seem futuristic. Consumers often ask how a wearable will help them live a better life. Companies that sell wearables must answer all the questions.

That is where marketers come in. They develop plans to inform the public about products. They create a desire in people to want to buy those wearables. Their focus is on **demographics**. That is the qualities of a specific group of people like their age, gender, and income.

Marketers target age groups most likely to be interested in a certain wearable. They would launch a marketing plan to sell a toy or game to children and teens. Their plan to market health-related devices would target adults. Highly expensive wearables would be marketed to wealthier consumers.

Marketing directors meet often with their marketing teams. These marketing specialists and managers discuss and

Imagine It!

- Think about any video game you find interesting.

- Imagine you are in marketing. Try to write a convincing radio commercial that would convince people to buy it. Write it so you can read it in fifteen seconds.

- Now write a headline about the game in eight words or less.

Dig Deeper!

- Keep a notebook handy the next time you watch cartoons.

- Write down catchy slogans in commercials used to convince kids they must have that product.

Marketing products involves lots of creative ideas.

compare ideas. They decide the best approaches to use each product. They provide instructions to those that write and create advertisements and run marketing campaigns. Marketers often travel to promote their wares.

They understand products and how to reach people in each demographic. Marketing plans to pitch wearable toys might target TV cartoon shows or websites for young people. Those that pitch products for medical use would target hospitals.

The rise of the Internet and social media have given marketers more options. Newspapers and magazines can now be found online. Marketers create plans to pitch products on websites that accept advertising. They also seek to create a positive image of every product on their company website.

Social media is especially popular. Marketers understand the incredible number of people that visit sites such as Facebook and Twitter.

Future Marketing Director

Marketing courses in high school and college teach students how to analyze and promote products. Those that yearn to market wearables should learn all about wearable technology. Gaining internships with wearable tech companies is a valuable tool in establishing a career.

Project Manager

The title sounds easy enough: project manager. A project manager manages projects, right? But the job is not that simple. Project managers take a big picture look at each project. They play a role in every aspect of a project from start to finish. They get a lot of credit if the project succeeds. But they take much of the blame if it fails.

Times have changed. Project managers were once handed an idea and told to run with it. Now they develop their own ideas. And in the emerging world of wearables, that could mean almost anything!

The idea is the first step. Project managers work with designers, engineers, and others professionals to deliver a finished product. Project managers might direct a plan involving anything from a virtual reality headset to a wrist band that detects cancer cells in the human body.

One important task is to organize a team that can turn an idea into reality. A big part of the job involves finding just the right person for each task. That means the project manager needs to know what it takes to do the job. And he or she needs to figure out the best person to get the job done on other projects as well.

Communication skills are critical. Project managers must make clear the tasks of every team member. They need

Imagine It!

➡ Imagine you are the project manager of a board game you have at home.

➡ Devise a plan to improve the game.

➡ Write down the changes and play the game with your addition.

Dig Deeper!

✔ It takes a team to do many things. For example, think of a typical day at school.

✔ Start with the people who get all the students to school and make a list of everyone who makes the day run smoothly.

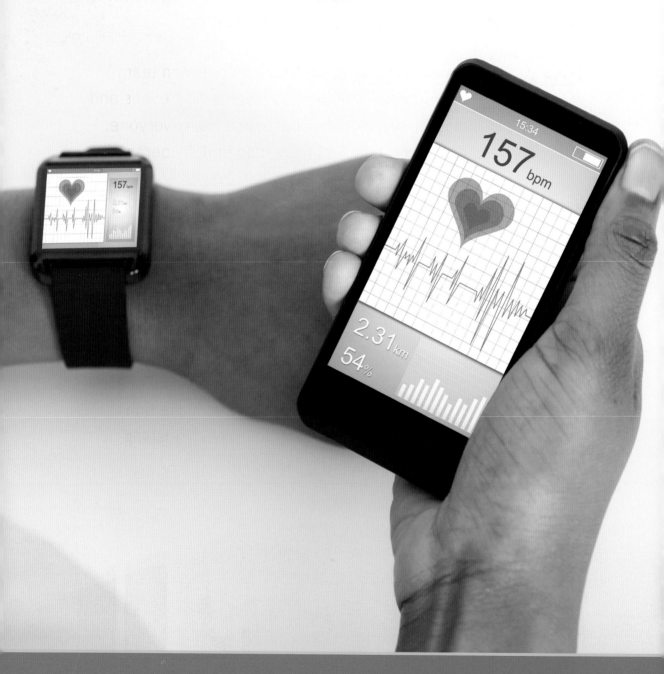

Product managers turn concepts into products.

to understand what they will be working on every day. The job also requires an ability to motivate. The project manager should instill a sense of excitement into each team member.

There will be bumps along the road. Conflicts between team members are natural. Project managers resolve differences and keep people happy. They motivate, coach, and train everyone. People work better when they feel respected and encouraged.

Project managers also keep costs down. They create a budget for each venture. They then manage the money to ensure they remain within that budget.

Perhaps a wearable toy costs more to produce than first estimated. Project managers must clear the cost with the company. Or they must find a way to lower cost in another area.

The final step is showing your work to those that make final decisions. Your team is proud of what it achieved. Finishing a project is a satisfying moment for project managers.

Future Project Manager

Project managers need at least a bachelor's degree. But they have options. They can major in management, business, or another related field. They must be very organized with the personality to motivate others.

Can You Imagine?

Innovation always starts with an idea. This was true for Alexander Graham Bell, Thomas Edison, Henry Ford, and the Wright brothers. It is still true today as innovators imagine new forms of wearable technology. And it will still be true in the future when you begin your high-tech career. So ...

What is your big idea?

Think of a cool new way to use wearable technology. Write a story or draw a picture to share your idea with others.

Please do **NOT** write in this book if it doesn't belong to you.
Gather your own paper and art supplies and get creative with your ideas!

Glossary

artificial intelligence (ahr-tuh-FISH-uhl in-TEL-ih-juhns) the ability of a digital computer or computer-controlled robot to perform tasks commonly associated with humans

components (kuhm-POH-nuhnts) parts of a computer or other type of technology device

consumer (kuhn-SOO-mur) person who buys a product or service for their own personal use

demographics (dem-uh-GRAF-iks) information about specific groups of people that is used to help develop products that certain types of people will buy

robot (ROH-baht) a machine that is programmed to perform complex human tasks

statistics (stuh-TIS-tiks) facts or pieces of information taken from a study that cover a much larger quantity of information

virtual reality (VUR-choo-uhl ree-AL-ih-tee) a computer-created environment that looks and seems real to the person who experiences it

visual perception (VIZH-oo-uhl pur-SEP-shuhn) the ability to see and give meaning to the visual information that surrounds us

wearable electronics (WAIR-uh-buhl ih-lek-TRAH-niks) technology that can be worn on the body as an accessory or part of material used in clothing

Index

About the Author

Martin Gitlin is a freelance author based in Cleveland. He has had more than 110 books published. He won more than 45 writing awards during his 11 years as a newspaper journalist, including first place for general excellence from the Associated Press. That organization selected him as one of the top four feature writers in Ohio in 2001.